Returning from Epsom Races down Sutton High Street

SUTTON
A Pictorial History

Angel Cutting and Bridge

SUTTON
A Pictorial History

Frank Burgess

Phillimore

1993

Published by
PHILLIMORE & CO. LTD.
Shopwyke Manor Barn, Chichester, Sussex

ISBN 0 85033 855 7

Printed and bound in Great Britain by
BIDDLES LTD.
Guildford, Surrey

To the staff, past and present, of the Heritage Department of the Central Library of Sutton, in appreciation of their willing co-operation and friendship over a period of twenty years.

List of Illustrations

Frontispiece. Angel cutting and bridge

Illustration Acknowledgements

The illustrations are from two sources only.
From the collection in the Heritage Archive of the London Borough of Sutton: 2, 4-7, 9-16, 18, 19, 22-36, 38, 39, 41, 42, 43, 45, 46, 47, 50-66, 68-79, 81-87, 89-93, 95, 96, 97, 100-103, 108, 109-112, 114-116, 118-122, 124-130, 135-140, 142-157, 165, 167-178.
From the author's own collection: 1, 3, 8, 17, 20, 21, 37, 40, 44, 48, 49, 67, 80, 88, 94, 98, 99, 104-107, 113, 117, 123, 131-134, 141, 155, 158-164, 166.

Acknowledgements

I am very conscious of the invaluable and willing assistance which I have received and which has made possible the production of this book. Firstly, I acknowledge with grateful thanks Mr. Peter Smithson, Director of Leisure Services of the London Borough of Sutton, for his permission to use photographs and illustrations from his department's collection; Miss June Broughton, Assistant Heritage Officer, for her help in selecting the material and for reading through my manuscript and making valuable suggestions and corrections. My thanks also to the members of her staff who were ever willing to search out and satisfy my many queries. I am also greatly indebted to my typist, Valary Murphy, who gave up her spare time to decipher my manuscript and so competently type the whole 'story'.

I thank Mr. Arthur Pearson for his permission to use photograph no. 98 and for the detailed history of his family's business. Finally, I gratefully acknowledge with love my wife's patience during the many hours when I dwelt in the past whilst compiling this book.

FRANK BURGESS

CHEAM 1993

Introduction

The Development of the Town

The present name 'Sutton' applies to the London Borough of that name, founded in 1965 by the amalgamation of the Borough of Sutton and Cheam, the Borough of Beddington and Wallington, and Carshalton Urban District. Most of the illustrations in this book precede this event by over half a century and so are confined to the town of Sutton itself.

Administratively Sutton originated as a local board in 1882, and was created an Urban District in 1894. Cheam, a parish of Epsom Rural District, was added in 1928, creating Sutton and Cheam U.D.C. This authority was incorporated by Royal Charter in 1934, making it a Municipal Borough. It became a Parliamentary Borough in 1945.

The parish of Sutton is one of the 'finger parishes'; Cuddington, Cheam, Sutton, Carshalton and Beddington are so called because they are long from north to south and narrow from east to west. The southern part is on chalk and the north on London clay, with a narrow belt of sand in between. It was on this water-bearing sand that the villages were established, surrounded by the cultivated farmland with common grazing to the north, and open downland to the south. Although Sutton common was enclosed in 1809, the downs to the south are still open and under the control of the Banstead Commons Conservators.

Sutton parish stretched from the foot of the downs at Belmont to Rosehill in the north; a distance of three and a half miles. Until the turn of the century Sutton was a 'one street town' on the road from London to the south. In 1755 an east-west road from Croydon to Ewell and Epsom had been opened, but this did not form part of the village until much later. Until 1882 both these roads were turnpikes with tollgates which were originally at the crossroads at the *Cock Hotel* but were later moved, one to Brighton Road, near Sutton Lodge farm, and the other into Cheam Road at the junction with York Road.

In 1847 the railway arrived and, from that time onwards, things began to change. The village developed and ultimately became a thriving town. Easy and rapid access to and from the City of London made it a desirable residential area for city workers and housing developments proliferated. This created the need for development in other spheres such as retail and the service industries, blacksmiths, farriers, saddlers and the like, and most noticeably for larger places of worship. The parish church of St Nicholas was rebuilt in 1864, Benhilton was created as a new parish and All Saints' church was built in 1866. This was followed 10 years later by Christ Church in 1876, and St Barnabas church in 1884.

Other denominations built larger substantial edifices thus confirming the population 'explosion': Baptists in 1886, Congregational in 1888, Methodists in 1884 and Roman Catholics in 1892. In the 40 years after the coming of the railway the population had increased tenfold, from 1,387 in 1851 to 13,977 in 1891, and in the next 40 years it more than doubled again to 27,978.

This expansion had also been aided by the provision of public services. Sutton Gas Company was founded in 1857, the Water Company in 1864, the Electricity Company in 1899, and in 1906 the electric tram service to Croydon was opened. Also during this period an extensive drainage system was installed with a sewage treatment works on the side of the Pylbrook.

Another factor which facilitated the construction of houses was the availability of bricks. Brick-making requires clay, sand and water, all of which were available locally; at one time there were six brickfields in or about the village.

Although the railway was the first stimulus to progress, the general transport was still the horse-drawn vehicle which reigned until the advent of the motorcar at the beginning of the present century.

Before the road from Redhill to Horley was opened, the main route to Brighton was through Sutton and Reigate. In 1845 as many as 20 coaches a day changed horses at the *Cock Hotel* on their way to and from the south coast. In addition, many carriers' wagons passed through, carrying fish from the coast or country produce up to the London markets.

Sutton formed one of the main approaches to the downs, and on Epsom racedays it is said that traffic was solid from the tollgate in the Brighton Road through the village to Rosehill. The higher part of the High Street was fairly steep, and cock-horses were available at the *Greyhound* yard to assist heavily loaded vehicles up the hill. There is evidence that, in the latter part of the 18th century, the gradient was eased as it crossed the Carshalton to Cheam road. The resulting dip in this road as it crosses High Street can be seen today. In 1936 when traffic signals were proposed for these crossroads, horses were still being used by the coal merchants and other heavy hauliers. They raised great objections to the proposal because, in the event of their horses being obliged to stop at a red light on this steep part of the hill, they would find it very difficult if not impossible to start off again.

In the days when dray-horses were in common use, the state of the roads was affected in two ways. Firstly their construction had to provide a good non-slip surface, which was known as waterbound macadam. This was muddy in winter and dusty in summer, and the horses themselves added further to the filthy state of the carriageways. It was not until the early days of this century that experiments with tarmacadam were made on the Brighton road, and from then on the town roads became progressively cleaner as waterbound macadam gave way to tarred surfaces and the number of horses declined.

Many early writers on Sutton have mentioned the atrocious state of the roads, particularly the quagmires between Rosehill and Angel Hill. This was improved sometime in the 19th century by the construction of a causeway some six or eight feet high across this low-lying land, perhaps by using material from the excavation of the Angel cutting.

The area was also noted for its well-wooded aspect. There was not only Benhill Wood immediately to the north of the village, but the High Street is said to have had trees overhanging from adjacent land and gardens for its whole length, which is exactly a mile from the Green to the railway bridge, and rises one hundred feet. Although Benhill Wood largely disappeared in the middle of the last century to make way for houses, a few old oak trees still remain in the Oakhill Road and Benhill Road vicinity. One tree in High Street survived outside the site of the *Greyhound Hotel* until the night of the great storm of October 1987. Nevertheless the present town is still well endowed with trees of many varieties, a fact that is frequently remarked upon by visitors.

During the last war the 'one street' character of the town had one advantage: although the district received many hundreds of German bombs there were only three major incidents in the shopping street itself. Two were unexploded bombs, one of which exploded the next morning and demolished the property next to the *Green Man* public house; the other was removed by the bomb disposal squad. The third incident was the most serious: a flying bomb fell at the end of Vale Road early one morning, causing a number of casualties.

It is interesting to note how the centre of business has moved up and down the street throughout the years of development. At first the village was centred at the north end near the Green, the rest of the street being largely residential and open land. As development took place these gave way to shops, first up as far as Benhill Street, and later up the hill to the station, which it had reached by 1870. During this period the centre of commerce ascended the hill, and that at the lower part of the street tended to die. By the 1930s the businesses above St Nicholas Road were predominant. This situation remained until the 1950s, when business began to drift down again to West Street, where it remained for the next 30 years. During the 1980s it moved further down still, and the greatest focus is currently between West Street and Marshalls Road, with trade in the higher part of the street being less busy.

A redevelopment plan was drawn up in 1963 and it has been progressively implemented since. The main feature of this plan was the provision of a parallel road on each side of the High Street, enabling vehicular traffic to be routed out of the shopping street which could then be given over to pedestrians. This was achieved in the late 1980s although this is not to say that development is complete, and what the future holds remains to be seen.

Early Views

1. This cutting from the *Sutton Journal* of 1865 refers to Mr. Lewis Hind's contemporary photographs, thereby confirming the age of these first few illustrations as the earliest surviving photographs of the village.

OUR VILLAGE IN PHOTOGRAPH.—Mr. Wm. Lewis Hind has just published, under the above title, a series of views of Sutton. They are larger in size than ordinary, ranging with the view of the Parish Church exhibited by him in a frame some time since at the Station, but are offered at a moderate price. The views embrace the High-street from different points, the Church, the Metropolitan Schools, the National Schools, the old and picturesque scenery of the Carshalton-road chalk-pit, and other favourite spots, new and old. Not the least interesting amongst them is the view of Mrs. Green's cottage in Church-lane. This cottage is well remembered by many as the old village school, where, in childhood, the first rudiments of knowledge were learnt. Mr. Hind has succeeded, not only in producing a series of most excellent photographs, but, with true artistic taste and skill, has made each scene a picture, which, apart from its local interest, bespeaks attention as a work of art. Thus they are interesting to the public at large, whilst they will be specially prized by those who possess them in years to come as mementos of what Sutton, now so rapidly changing, once was.—"SUTTON JOURNAL," July 12, 1865.

2. Lucy Green's cottage. Careful scrutiny shows a little girl with the man at the wellhead, another amongst the flowers and a row of faces in the right-hand window. Not to be missed is the row of boys' heads looking over the church fence on the left.

3. The new St Nicholas church. This picture was taken shortly after its completion in 1864.

4. Oliver Brown's butcher's shop halfway down the High Street. In 1865 the meat was displayed in the open shopfront in complete disregard of the filthy state of the roadway which was notoriously dusty in summer. Before the days of coldroom storage the only concession to hygiene was the overhead canopy to keep the sun off the meat.

5. The High Street outside the *Greyhound Inn*. The beam across the road was to carry the sign of the *Greyhound*. This picture clearly illustrates the poor state of the highway. The canopy of Brown's butcher's shop can be seen beyond the cart.

6. One of Mr. Hind's less clear photographs shows the entrance to Pearson's smithy, with West Street corner in the centre of the picture. The wagonette is believed to be on its way to Box Hill with a picnic party.

7. This picture of the High Street shows George Barnes' veterinarian forge and ironmonger's shop in the foreground (opposite what later became Manor Place). Before the days of veterinary surgeons, farriers did their work.

8. George Barnes' trade card showing some of his specialities including 'Patent Ashplate Felt' (sic) which on the shop poster is advertised at 'one penny a yard'. It also tells us that the family firm had been established for over a hundred years when the photograph was taken in 1865.

ESTABLISHED 1759.

Lawn Mowing Machines. Garden Tools & Rollers.

Geo. BARNES,

Furnishing Ironmonger & General Smith,

High Street,

Kitchen Furniture Rep'd & Tin'd. Lacquering & Bronzing.

SUTTON, SURREY,

BELLHANGER, LOCKSMITH & GAS-FITTER,

MANUFACTURER OF REGISTER & GAS STOVES, KITCHEN RANGES,

Hot & Cold Water Pipes fitted to Baths, Hothouses, Conservatories &c.

Baths for Sale or Hire. ORNAMENTAL IRON FENCE, TOMB RAILING,

Strained Wire Fence & Wire Netting. Patent Ashplate Felt.

HORSES CAREFULLY SHOD.

9. The third generation of the Barnes family, taken in 1886 in the backyard of their house in West Street.

10. This picture of Sutton police station, in the High Street was taken in 1854 alongside the entrance to the flour mill which stood behind the station. This building was vacated in 1909 when the new station was built in Carshalton Road (*see* plate 42), and was converted into a shop by Dendy Napper, the miller (*see* plate 84).

11.   The beam over the road carrying the sign of the *Cock Hotel* (which is out of sight round the right-hand corner). The photograph must have been taken *c.*1870 because the terraced shops in the middle distance, which were built in that year, have not yet had their shopfronts fitted. On the left is the *Railway Tavern*, now the *Green Man*, and beyond the cart is the entrance to Cheam Road.

12. Mr. Potter's butcher's shop, with the meat hanging in the open air, was situated on the corner of the entrance to the gasworks, where Eagle Star House now stands.

13. This picture shows the pond in West Street, known as Diver's Ditch, which filled up whenever the bourne water rose, and overflowed northwards to join the headwaters of the Pylbrook at the back of the Green. According to C. J. Marshall the pond was filled up in 1866.

14. We have seen the last of Mr. Hind's photographs, but this and plate 15 are thought to be contemporary with them, and show the Manor and its grounds. It is seen here from the front with the stables to the right.

15. The Manor was demolished in 1896 and the grounds shown here were sold off and developed. The houses which still stand in Lenham Road, Litchfield Road and Warwick Road form part of this development.

Churches and Chapels

16. This 1790 drawing of St Nicholas' church shows the original wooden tower which was replaced *c.*1800 with a brick one.

17. It is interesting to note that the artists of both these views include Lucy Green's cottage on the left-hand side and the end of the tithe barn on the right.

18. This 1806 view of St Nicholas' church contains considerable artistic licence. Although the church building is reasonably correct and the Gibson tomb shown in its true position, the whole is depicted isolated on a hill, whereas in reality it is in a depression, and neither the tithe barn nor the school cottage is depicted.

19. A good view of the new church in 1890. This building replaced the one shown in the three preceding illustrations in 1864 and remains standing today.

20.   This building was the early Wesleyan Methodist chapel in Clifton Crescent in Benhill Avenue, built well back on the site to enable it to be incorporated in a larger church built in front when finances permitted. In the event the Methodists sold the site to the Salvation Army, building a larger church in Carshalton Road (*see* plate 25).

21.   The Congregational Mission church in Benhill Street was built in 1859 and included schoolrooms at the rear. Although this building survived until the 1980s, the Congregationalists transferred to their new church built in Carshalton Road in 1888 (*see* plate 25).

22.   In 1907 the Methodists built their present church on the corner of St Nicholas Road and Cheam Road and vacated that
shown in plate 26. This photograph was taken after the opening ceremony when the attendant crowd was allowed to enter.

23. This photograph of 1913 shows the new Trinity Methodist church and its fine complex of halls on the corner of Hill Road.

24. A view of Carshalton Road showing the Congregational church in the foreground and the high roof of the Methodist church in the centre. The round house in the centre was often described, erroneously it is now believed, as the Carshalton Road tollhouse.

25. The fine detail of the Congregational church, built in 1888 and demolished in 1976, can be seen in this photograph.

26. The Wesleyan Methodist church in Carshalton Road was built in 1884 and vacated in 1907, after which it became an electric cinema called Sutton Hippodrome and later still an engineering works which continued in business into the 1950s.

27. The Baptists' first purpose-built meeting-room in Carshalton Road, *c*.1862. This was used as their chapel until they built a large church in 1886 on the corner of Hill Road and High Street. During the First World War the ladies of St Barnabas church used the meeting-room as a 'Soldiers Welcome' and it still exists today as a servicemen's club.

28. In 1883 the Baptists first developed their new site in Hill Road by building a schoolroom-cum-chapel, shown here in the foreground. This was followed by the church in 1886.

29. This view shows how the Baptist church stood on the corner of Hill Road and High Street until 1934 when Mr. Shinner bought it to enable him to extend his store (*see* plate 80).

Public Buildings

30. The municipal offices were built in 1900 in High Street on the corner of Throwley Road at a cost of £8,372. They served the town well for 70 years, being demolished in 1971.

31. Sutton Public Hall, which was built as a private venture in 1878 at a cost of £3,700, included a small hall at the rear and a number of ancillary rooms which were rented by the local authority as offices until 1900, when the municipal offices were built. During the same period, the fire brigade was also stationed here, as the fire escape shed shows. The council eventually purchased the hall in 1920 and it was the centre of the town's social activities for over 60 years until it was demolished in 1981.

32. This view of Throwley Road *c*.1910 shows the flank of the new municipal offices with the fire station alongside them in the centre and the County School for Boys, built in 1899, in the foreground.

33. At one time there were three separate fire brigades in the town. This one was the New Town volunteer brigade, shown at its appliance house in Vernon Road in 1890. It was established because the residents of New Town felt too remote from the other two brigades centred in the High Street.

34.   The town's volunteer brigade was formed in 1875 and is shown here in the stable yard of the *Cock Hotel*. Both volunteer brigades had manual pumps drawn by tradesmen's horses or, in the case of the town brigade, by dustcart horses, which, at the sound of the steam whistle of the flour mill, 'dropped everything', so to speak, and galloped off to pick up the fire appliances.

35.   The third brigade was that of the local board, formed in 1874 and shown here in Edward Terrace in the High Street. At first the brigade had manual pumps, but the steam pump shown was purchased in 1875. It was, of course, still drawn by 'volunteer' horses.

36.   Between 1879 and 1901 the brigade was stationed at the Public Hall, and this picture shows the steam pump standing outside the Hall. The pump was housed in the basement below the stage, outside the doors of which it is standing in this picture.

37. The post office in Grove Road, built c.1907, succeeded one at 14 High Street. Judging by the model of the motorcycle at the kerb, the photograph was probably taken in the early 1920s.

The Post Office, Sutton.

38. This is a later photograph of the post office and the new telephone exchange which was built alongside in 1929. Later still, they were both enlarged and modernised. Whilst the refurbishment was in progress, post office counter business was conducted at the building on the corner of Grove Road and Sutton Park Road. It is worth noting the row of trees, which was a feature of Grove Road for its whole length, extending right to the High Street (*see* plates 110 and 111).

39. The public baths in Throwley Road, built in 1903 at a cost of £6,754, included slipper baths for men and women as well as the very popular swimming bath. The building was demolished in 1971.

40. The interior of the swimming pool, showing the changing cubicles on either side. In the early days, male and female swimming sessions were held separately, but in later years when they were held jointly ladies used the cubicles on one side and men those on the other, and even the pool-side walks were out of bounds to the opposite sex.

41. The cottage hospital in Hill Road, built in 1901 at a cost of £2,800, succeeded a six-bed 'cottage' hospital in Bushey Road, and was itself succeeded by the present General Hospital in Chiltern Road in 1931.

42. The present police station in Carshalton Road, photographed shortly after it was built in 1909. Note the poster on the wall advertising for recruits.

43. The Sutton offices of the Wandsworth and District Gas Company in High Street, just below Crown Road. This photograph was taken *c.*1950 whilst the trolleybuses were still running, but after the street lamp had been converted to electricity from gas.

44. This was one of two identical houses in Cheam Road: Norfolk House and Suffolk House. The former, shown here, became an hotel until it was demolished in 1963. Suffolk House, visible on the left of the picture, still stands as part of the Sutton High School for Girls.

45. The Cheam Road Cinema, built in 1911 in a grandiose style presumably to attract the well-to-do, who could mount the rather grand steps direct from their carriages, but in later years it became known as the 'fleapit', and later still was named the Curzon. In the 1970s it was completely refurbished and renamed Studios 1.2.3. which was closed in 1992. It was preceded by three early cinemas, the Bioscope and Sutton Electric Cinema, both in High Street, and Sutton Hippodrome in Carshalton Road.

46. The modern cinema built in Carshalton Road in 1934 started life as the Plaza. In 1942 its name was changed to Granada which was closed in 1979 and an office block was built on the site It had a large restaurant with musicians' gallery, and was a popular venue for a meal. It was also available for private functions including dances.

7.   The Surrey County Cinema in High Street. It was built in 1920 and renamed the Gaumont before being demolished in 1959.

48. Sutton roller skating rink, known as the Gliderdrome, in Throwley Road. Built in 1909 for use with steel-wheeled skates, it was later converted to a billiard hall, and was reconverted in 1936 for use with rubber-wheeled skates. Closed in 1939, it became the food office for the duration of the war.

49. The interior of the skating rink *c*.1938, which was claimed to be the largest rink in the country.

50. The tithe barn and tithe keeper's cottage alongside St Nicholas' churchyard. The barn appears in a drawing of 1790 (*see* plate 16), and here it is shown a century and a half later, shortly before it was demolished to make way for garages for wartime vehicles. It stood on the line of the present Gibson Road.

51. The bandstand which stood in Manor Park. It was last used during and immediately after the Second World War for the 'Holidays at Home' movement, when our coastal resorts were closed to visitors, and travel was restricted elsewhere. Vandals made it unsafe and it was demolished in the 1950s.

High Street

52. The top of High Street viewed from Brighton Road across the station bridge in 1912. On the left (in the entrance to Mulgrave Road) can be seen the drinking fountain and behind it a horse trough. When the public fountain was no longer used it was demolished and the horse trough, which was still a much-needed asset, was removed to Brighton Road near to the coal yard entrance.

53. Looking down High Street from the station bridge in 1920 before Bowling's the ironmonger had left the corner on the right and opened a new shop in Grove Road. Apart from the street scene, the buildings are very little changed today.

54. This is facing south along the same length of High Street as shown in the previous picture. From the attitude of the shoppers, it is obviously not a rainy day, so the wet road suggests that a watering-cart had recently passed by, possibly having filled up at the curved standpipe to be seen on the right in the entrance to Grove Road. Wootton Brothers was a high-class drapers, opened in 1822, and much esteemed by the ladies of Sutton.

55. A view down the High Street over the Carshalton to Cheam Road crossing in 1925, with a police constable on point duty. William Pile's enlarged shop with its clock in its lead-covered cupola can be seen standing on the corner of Carshalton Road.

56. The same view in 1938. Electric traffic signals had replaced the policeman on point duty two years earlier, and the Electricity Board had built new premises in place of the South Met building shown in the previous illustration. The photo also provides a good view of the *Cock Hotel* sign, which is still a prominent feature of the town today.

57. The length of the High Street known as Cock Hill in 1890, 10 years after the buildings on the right were completed. Those on the left were built 10 years earlier still, in 1870. There is a notable lack of traffic, but the dirty highway is surprising for the main shopping street of the town.

58. The same part of High Street 12 years later, in 1902, showing very little change.

59. J. Sainsbury's shop in High Street. This building had previously been the first bank in the town, and permission to convert it to a shop was sought by J. Sainsbury Esquire in 1896. It was one of his earliest branches and trade continued there until 1960. In the distance, beyond the Baptist church, can be seen the terrace of old shops occupied progressively by Ernest Shinner (*see* plates 77, 78, 79).

60. A closer view of the Baptist church on the corner of Hill Road in 1932, after Mr. Shinner had clad his old buildings with a new faience tile façade.

61. The municipal offices in 1902 on the corner of Throwley Road two years after they were built, with a distant view of trees overhanging the High Street.

62. Looking up Cock Hill, *c.*1920, past the municipal offices to the Prudential building at the top, standing on the site of the old *Cock Hotel*.

63. In the early years of this century, there were nearly as many boot and shoe shops in the High Street as there are today, and this is one of them: Robert Stevens' shop *c.*1900. Walter Stevens also had shoe shops at 23 and 91 High Street, the former retaining the name until the 1970s.

64. The same premises some ten years later, showing the deterioration which often occurred before redevelopment took place. The small, single-storey corner building has been thought to be an early tollhouse, but photographic evidence shows this to be unlikely.

65.   In this 1890 view of High Street, the white-walled entrance to Tom Pearson's blacksmith shop, established in 1850, can be seen on the right and, on the other side, is the sign of the three balls of Herrington the pawnbroker. In the distance, under the *Greyhound* sign beam, can be seen a flock of sheep probably being taken to one of the butchers' slaughterhouses, either Oliver Brown's (*see* plates 4 and 172) or Henry Stevens' on the corner of Benhill Street (*see* plate 91).

66.   This photograph taken in 1928 includes a view of the beam across the street, carrying the sign of the *Greyhound*, which can be seen clearly. The beam remained until 1938, when it was removed to enable the carriageway to be widened.

67. One of the nicest views of Sutton High Street in the days before development had necessitated the removal of the trees. This picture was taken, *c.*1875, outside the *Greyhound Inn* looking down the street past Manor Lane on the right.

68. This is almost the same section of the street as that shown in plate 66, but taken 25 years later, in 1900. Most of the foreground buildings have been replaced, with the exception of the tall one, which remains standing; for many years it was a well-liked grocer's shop called Kingham's. The two-horse covered wagon probably belonged to one of the local carriers who plied daily to the metropolis.

69. On the right-hand side of this picture is the brick wall of the Manor grounds with the garden trees overhanging the High Street. Opposite is Frost's the chemist (the shop without a blind). This was an old-established pharmacy with three large coloured flasks in the window, well remembered by many older residents of the town.

70. An advertisement for one of Mr. Frost's specialities.

71. The High Street near the junction of Benhill Street, opposite which is the milestone which read 'Royal Exchange 12M. Whitehall 11½M' until it was defaced in 1940, when all such signs and place-names were obliterated preparatory to a possible German invasion.

72. A typical street scene in the early part of this century, showing a predominance of pedal cycles over the motorcars, one of which is just disappearing out of the picture. Pedestrians could cross the street safely. Haddon Road is shown leaving the High Street on the left.

High Street, Sutton.   20640A

73. Old cottages in High Street, on the bend opposite Crown Road, with the ruin of the town lock-up on their right, *c*.1910.

74. The same cottages as in the previous picture but looking south around the bend to the new *Red Lion* public house, built in 1907 alongside an older pub with the same name. In the early days of photography, a camera was a source of great curiosity, as shown by the lads in the foreground. The sign above the cottage door is that of one of the many local chimney sweeps, which in the days of domestic coal fires provided an essential service.

5. The very bottom of the High Street, approaching the Green, in 1896, with the tower of All Saints' church, Benhilton, prominent above the single-storey *Cricketers Inn*, which still stands opposite Bushey Road.

6. Three of the old shops which stood in the lower part of the High Street. The last of these was only demolished in the 1980s, preparatory to the building of a large Tesco store.

Shops and Workshops

77. In 1899 Ernest Shinner opened this shop at 79 High Street – it was the birth of the town's largest store.

78. Mr. Shinner's business was successful enough to enable him to buy the neighbouring shops progressively until he had all the terrace but one: Amos Reynolds' shop on the corner of St Nicholas Road.

79. Shinner's 28th anniversary sale. He was renowned for having frequent sales for one reason or another.

80. Between 1928 and 1934 Mr. Shinner clad the old terrace with a whole new shopfront as shown here on the right. This photograph was taken in 1934, the year when Mr. Shinner bought the Baptist church and extended his store up to the corner of Hill Road, and the Baptists built their fine new church in Cheam Road. The store was taken over by Messrs. Allders in the 1980s, and finally closed in 1992 when the business was transferred to the new St Nicholas Centre lower down the High Street.

81. This photograph of 1910 shows G. & R. Herrington's furniture store. It is especially interesting because it shows the early type of delivery vehicles used in the trade.

82. Similarly, this shows the typical two-wheeled butcher's delivery cart standing outside Oliver Brown's shop. Meat still hangs outside, as it had some fifty years before, as shown in plate 4.

83. On the corner of Carshalton Road and High Street stood another of Sutton's 'landmarks' – the shop belonging to William Pile. This served as bookshop, stationer, printer and seller of fancy goods. The building was erected in 1883 and this photograph was taken in 1903. Pile's closed in 1966, and the premises were taken over by the Electricity Company, until its demolition in 1987, when the Trustee Savings Bank was built.

84. Dendy Napper was the miller who owned and worked the steam roller flour mills which stood behind this shop. The building had previously been the police station (*see* plate 10) but was converted in 1909. This photograph of 1925 is interesting as it was returned to Sutton from Australia by an ex-employee of Napper's, who had taken it with him when he emigrated there upon his retirement. In his accompanying letter, he explained about what appear to be swagged pelmets in the windows. They were in fact fringes of ears of wheat, oats and barley which he had to renew each year after the harvests, by threading them on strings during the long winter evenings.

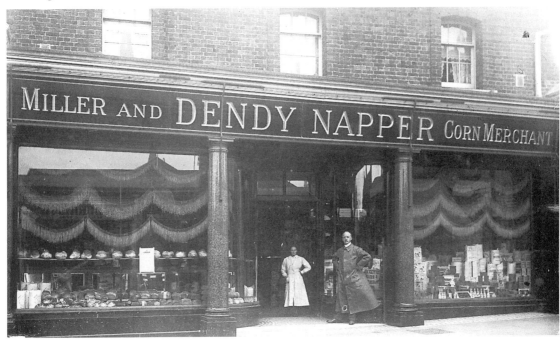

85. Hawkins' ironmonger's at 50 High Street. This is a good illustration of ironmonger's wares in the days when hand tools predominated, before the advent of power tools, when double-digging was the vogue, and lawnmowers were pushed by hand.

86. The Paragon 'high-class confectionery and tobacco'! The photograph was taken in 1957 when the old shop still projected beyond the modern frontage between James Walker jeweller's and Lilley & Skinner's shoe shop. After being cut back it became a modern 'heel bar'.

87. Short's dairy in Grove Road, *c.*1920. The Short family owned a farm in Carshalton. It was situated off Westmead Road, opposite the present Shorts Road, which was presumably named after them.

88. This picture of 1916 shows Short's milk 'pram' in St Nicholas Road alongside the Trinity Methodist church. During the First World War young ladies often took on the delivery rounds in the absence of men who were away in the trenches. It is noticeable that the glass bottles shown on the pram in 1920 are not yet in use.

89. W. Walker's sweet shop at 127 High Street. Although claiming to be a manufacturer of pure sweets, he apparently sold well-known brand makes also, such as Cadbury's, Pascall's, Velma, Rowntree's and Fry's.

90. Another sweet shop, this time in Lind Road New Town, not only selling White's ginger beer, but also White's hot drinks.

91. One of the two old-established butchers in the town was Henry Stevens on the corner of Benhill Street (the other was Oliver Brown). Stevens' slaughterhouse was situated at the rear of the shop, in Benhill Street. It was a member of the Stevens family who recovered and preserved the photographs of the Jubilee bullock shown in plates 171-72.

92. H. C. Stevens' delivery cart, a typical butcher's vehicle – similar to Brown's shown in plate 82.

93. W. J. Robins' motorcycle shop in Cliff Parade, Carshalton Road, *c*.1930. Note the old hand-operated semi-circular petrol pump on the left with its overhead swinging delivery pipe to serve vehicles at the kerbside.

94. The Viaduct cycle shop under new management at 66 High Street, *c*.1918. Clifton House was a flat above the shop, and the front door and the one next to it opened onto the foot of staircases. The shop is one of the row of bull-nosed shopfronts immediately below the municipal offices, which were later reconstructed as modern, flat, continuous shopfronts. The entrance to the flats above was transferred to the rear via the council offices yard.

95.   Amos Reynolds, the high-class furniture store and undertaker's on the corner of St Nicholas Road and High Street. Mr. Reynolds opened at 77 High Street in 1873, but later sold that shop to Mr. Shinner (*see* plate 78) and moved here.

96.   An interesting advertisement plate of Mr. Reynolds. The date is unknown, but the price range of Brussels carpet from 2s. 11d. to 3s. 9d. gives a clue to its antiquity.

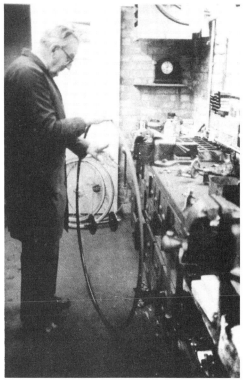

97. (*Above*) Pearson's family business is the oldest in the town still trading in its original premises; it started here as a blacksmith's in 1860. The forge closed in the 1880s, and converted to a bicycle workshop, which is still flourishing over a century later.

98. (*Above right*)Arthur Pearson, whose son runs the present shop, has had a life-long interest in penny farthing cycles, (in their day known as 'Ordinaries'). He is shown here building an 'Ordinary' front wheel in 1981.

99. (*Below*)The cycle workshop in the old forge at Pearson's.

100.   One of the principal garages in the town was Surrey Motors in Speedway House, St Nicholas Road. The noticeboard shows that they ran tours in early coaches known as charabancs. This developed into a modern coach business which ran until 1961, when the premises were demolished and the site redeveloped.

101.   W. Leeding's, which also developed into a modern garage business, started in 1823 as a carriage works, and is shown here at 89 High Street in the early days of motoring, c.1910, advertising Redline motor spirit and Mobiloil.

102.   This is an earlier view of Leeding's frontage. Their various carriages are being displayed for the photographer, probably in the early days of the camera, c.1860.

103.   Inside the carriage works yard again, with William Leeding (on the left) and his workforce posing for this photograph.

104 & 105. Another of the old-established family businesses was Montague Odd's, cricket bat makers. The bat willow was grown locally in the Pylbrook meadows, and the products were world renowned. These two photographs were taken in the workshop on the north side of West Street in the early part of the century. The business survived in a shed on the south side of the same street, making a few bats and restringing tennis rackets until *c.*1975, when it finally closed. The building now on the site is called Willow House.

106. Mr. Odd's interest in cricket, coupled with an eye for business, prompted him to erect this building as an indoor cricket school in Robin Hood Lane, opposite the end of West Street. Known as Surrey Cricket School it is today used as warehouse space.

107. This picture taken inside the cricket school shows three pitches in the nets and, surprisingly, a table tennis table at one side. The accommodation also included, on a first floor above the entrance hall, a lounge and bar for relaxation after practice.

Side Roads

108. Sutton is renowned for its trees and this avenue is in Christchurch Park. It was the threat to the trees on the right, caused by planned development of the land behind them, that led to the formation of the Sutton and Cheam Society for the preservation of local amenities. The society received so much support that the trees were saved and development was achieved without their destruction.

109. This is Cheam Road approaching the *Cock* crossroads, and is an example of what can be lost through the passage of time and unavoidable progress. Hardly any of these trees now remain, due to a combination of Dutch Elm disease and the requirements of traffic.

110. Grove Road in 1939, looking west towards Cheam. Grove Road was well-named as it was tree-lined from end to end and for most of its length remains so to this day. It has an unusual feature inasmuch as the trees are at the back of the path instead of at the kerbside.

111. This is the other 'face' of Grove Road in 1928; shops had been built on the front gardens of the old houses between Sutton Park Road and the High Street, but the row of trees remained until a later date, as they did on the other side of the road (*see* plate 38). Today not a tree remains in this length of Grove Road.

112. Cheam Road, *c.*1920. Sutton Boys' High School can be seen on the left and the cinema is opposite, with Trinity church spire above the trees. As so often happens on main roads in town centres, very few of the trees remain today.

113. This picture shows the same section of road as shown in the previous picture, but 30 years earlier, in 1890. The buildings to be seen on the left were replaced and eventually became part of the Boys' High School. It is interesting to note that on the right-hand path three young trees had recently been planted.

14 & 115.   These two residential roads, Sutton Park Road above and St Nicholas Road below, now form part of the southern gyratory traffic circuit and new parallel road system. Fortunately the trees in Sutton Park Road grow at the back of the path, and most of them have been saved.

116.   Snowdrop cottage and Crocus cottage in St Nicholas Road, next to the churchyard entrance, were built *c*.1880. The white cottage (Snowdrop) in the centre of the picture stood on the site of the village school shown in plate 2. The cottages were demolished in 1961 when Surrey Motors' site was redeveloped and the first section of St Nicholas Way was constructed.

117.   This cottage stood in St Nicholas Road where Surrey Motors' showrooms were built (*see* plate 100), and the street lamp is on the corner of High Street. The large trees in the background stood in the grounds of Doctor Herndon's house on the far side of High Street.

118.   This view of Robin Hood Lane from Cheam Road, *c.*1900, can no longer be seen, since the lane was closed and obliterated when the civic offices and central library were built, the trees on the left having been felled earlier when the car-park was constructed. Even the latter has now gone, replaced by the Holiday Inn.

119.   This is the lower end of Robin Hood Lane, which does still exist. Although the trees are gone, the sewer vent shaft is still there, and the footpath from the churchyard comes out on the right with Camden Road on the left. The *Robin Hood Inn* is just visible at the foot of the hill. It is not known whether the inn was named after the road, or vice versa.

120 & 121.   These two watercolours are by an unknown artist whose initials were A. W. W. They are of two of the Sutton tollhouses and gates in 1881, the year before the tolls were abolished. The one above is in Cheam Road, painted from Gander Green Lane, whilst the one below is in Brighton Road with Sutton Lodge farm in the distance.

122 & 123. In contrast to the toll roads era these two views are of Sutton bypass just after completion in 1928. The first picture shows Clensham Lane joining the bypass on the right. The lower picture has Stayton Road on the left and from this point as far as the eye can see the new road runs along the old line of Clensham Lane, which went as far as Gander Green Lane. At this time it was only a two lane carriageway but in 1938 work started on widening it to four lanes and adding cycle tracks. The work had only been completed as far south as Cheam railway bridge when war broke out and work ceased. It was never resumed after the war and the length from the railway to the downs is still two lanes without cycle tracks.

Transport

124.   Before 1906 the only public road transport was a horse bus service to Croydon. In that year electric trams were installed, and this picture shows one of the early open-topped trams at the Sutton terminus at the end of Benhill Street.

125. At all termini passengers congregate and vehicle crews require refreshment. This shows the Sutton Terminus Coffee & Dining Rooms in Benhill Street, which catered for such needs.

126. Later, as demand increased, covered double-decker trams were introduced, but they still had open staircases and no protection for the drivers.

127. In 1935 trolleybuses were introduced and for a little while, as shown here, they shared the routes with the trams. How they managed to share the trolley wires is a mystery. There is one fact, however, which is known and which influenced the routing in Sutton. The trams had terminated at the end of Benhill Street because they could not negotiate the sharp corner into High Street, but a tram did not need to turn around, as the driver simply drove from the other end. The trolleybuses however had to be able to turn round, and as they could manage the corner into High Street, albeit with a squealing of tyres, trolleybuses continued to the end of Bushey Road where they could turn.

128. Open-topped omnibuses passing the *Cock Hotel*, c.1925. Apparently even in those days they travelled in convoys!

129. Here is a trolleybus in Benhill Avenue alongside the *Grapes Hotel*. The destination blind says 'Crystal Palace' rather prematurely, since the driver has not yet been down to the Green to turn around. Habits have not changed much over the years.

130. The second railway station at Sutton, built in 1865, replaced a much more modest one, which was a couple of hundred yards along the up line. When it was closed, the small all-purpose wooden station building was acquired by Sutton Cricket Club, where it stands today as the scorer's and implement shed.

131. This is the third station, shown on the bridge at street level. It was built in 1885 and this photograph was taken in 1891.

132 & 133. These two illustrations show the Terrier locomotives which were in common use on the London, Brighton and South Coast Railway system. The one above is standing at the down platform at Sutton, *c.*1900. The lower one shows the original engine named *Sutton*. At present the borough council owns a similar engine of the same name which is in the care of East Kent Railway Preservation Society and is often to be seen in steam at Tenterden.

From CHEAM ROAD

134. In 1928 work commenced on a new line between Sutton and Wimbledon. Here a steam digger excavates the cutting between Grove Road and Cheam Road. At first, work went on 24 hours a day, but the local residents were so disturbed that they had to obtain an injunction to stop the contractor doing noisy work at night!

135. Here is another steam digger in the cutting approaching Sutton Common Road. Cheam church spire can be seen on the horizon. Both these photographs show construction wagons on the temporary ways before the permanent way is laid.

Public Houses

136. To previous generations Sutton has been symbolised by the *Cock Hotel*, which stood at the top of the village street where the Croydon to Epsom road crossed. This is the oldest illustration of the building known to exist. It was painted by Thomas Rowlandson in 1790, looking through the tollgate, under the sign on its beam, with the little tollhouse to the right on the corner of Cheam Road.

137. A good view of the hotel, one hundred years later in 1890, with the beerhouse on the left known as the *Cock Tap*. By now, all evidence of the tollgate had gone. Although the tolls were not abolished until 1882 the gates had been removed from here in 1863 (*see* plates 120-21).

138. In 1896 the old *Tap* beerhouse was demolished and on the site a large modern hotel was built before the old hotel was pulled down. Here the new one is shown immediately after its opening, with the old hotel standing in the background. The young tree in the right foreground appears to be one of those shown in plate 113.

139. This 1932 view of the 'new' *Cock Hotel* shows the sign in the centre of the road, where it is today. Originally it stood on the path in front of the hotel, just where the man in this picture is stepping onto the footpath. The column originally carried two gas lanterns below the sign, the pipes for which still exist but now carry the local direction signs.

140. The two public houses shown on this page stood at the extreme opposite ends of the Sutton district. *The Plough* in Sutton Common Road, shown above *c.*1900, was replaced by a more modern one which was demolished by a German bomb at closing time one night in 1942. The present building was erected in 1959. It was an ironic coincidence that its namesake in Gander Green Lane was also hit on the same night at closing time.

141. The *California* in Brighton Road, Belmont, was also demolished by a direct hit at closing time one night, resulting in many casualties and the award of bravery medals to rescue party members. Some of the ruins were salvaged and refurbished as a single-storey building. In this form it served its patrons until a modern replacement was built behind and renamed the *Belmont*.

142. *The Grapes Hotel* in 1906. It was built on the corner of Benhill Street and High Street in 1896. It does not seem to have attracted the coach trade, as by this time the railways played a more important role. It has, however, been a prominent feature of the town, being the 'landmark' destination of the trams from Crystal Palace and Croydon. It has changed its character a number of times in recent years, and is currently called *The Corner House*.

143. The *Blackwater Tavern* was a small inn in Blackwater Road, a quiet street off the High Street. It was formed originally from one of a pair of semi-detached cottages and in 1937 it was enlarged by the conversion of the other cottage. It was demolished in 1991 preparatory to the construction of the St Nicholas Centre and multi-storey car-park.

144. *The Cricketers*, named presumably because it is in the vicinity of the Green where cricket was played, is mainly a timber-clad building. It was erected in 1790, and a brick single-storey front was added in the early part of this century. It was further enlarged in 1972, and is a Grade II listed building.

145.   The *Greyhound Hotel* in High Street was one of the stagecoach hostelries in the village. It was one of only two inns whose sign was carried on a beam across the street. The building shown here replaced the original in 1873 and was itself demolished in 1959. The beam was removed in 1938 but the tree in the centre of the picture remained until the night of the great storm of 1987.

146. The *Red Lion* in High Street was built in 1907 alongside its predecessor. Both pubs are shown here, and this picture dates from *c.*1908, before the old one was demolished. Demolition left a small, unused, fenced-off site which remained until the last war. In 1941 an unexploded bomb hole was discovered in this vacant land alongside the inn, and great excitement was occasioned when it was realised that the bomb was one of a 'stick' which had been dropped 10 days earlier, and the danger of explosion had existed for that time. It was removed safely by the army's bomb disposal squad.

147. In the distance is the original *Windsor Castle* public house in Lind Road, opposite the end of Vernon Road. In 1870 shortly after the photograph was taken the building, which stood on ground acquired by the newly-formed water company, was demolished and the name and business transferred to a shop premises in Greyhound Road on the corner of Myrtle Road, where it remains today.

148. New Town was the name given to a development in Sutton which took place in the 19th century and was well established when this hotel was built in 1870, taking the name *New Town Hotel*, later condensed to the *New Town*. This photograph can be dated to *c*.1970 from the style of the street lamp columns and from the fact that the adjoining house was incorporated in the hotel in 1977.

149. *The Cross Keys* was the smallest beer-house in the town until it closed in 1956. It stood in Vernon Road, next to the corner shop in William Road. The premises still exist as a cottage.

Further Views

150. Sutton Green, *c*.1910, at the corner of Bushey Road and the beginning of London Road and Angel Hill. The Green was awarded to the residents of the village under the Sutton Common Enclosure Award in 1810. The row of elm trees in the centre of the picture formed the eastern boundary of the common, and remained there until devastated by Dutch elm disease in the early 1970s.

151. The Green from Bushey Road in 1898; the little row of shrubs in the foreground had recently been planted. Their subsequent growth is an aid to the dating of later photographs. The large house on the left of the picture was Elmsleigh in London Road, which was used later in life by Amos Reynolds as a furniture repository (*see* plates 95-96).

152. The Green pond in 1928. This was on the south corner of Bushey Road and High Street and is seen here from its south-west corner, looking across Bushey Road to the Green itself. What looks like a series of arches of a viaduct is in fact the shrubs mentioned under the previous plate, some 30 years later.

153.   Another view of the pond, taken by Francis Frith and Company in 1898, showing the *Cricketers Inn* on the left and the buildings at the beginning of High Street on the right. The tree growing on the island was planted in 1837, to commemorate the coronation of Queen Victoria. During the Second World War the pond served as an emergency water supply for fire-fighting. In 1955 it was filled in and turned into a small rest garden.

154. One of the delightful features of old Sutton was Angel cutting with the ornamental bridge across from Sutton Common Road to All Saints Road. This photograph taken in 1891 shows the beauty of the spot in the days when traffic was minimal. In 1937 when traffic had increased, one of the brick supports cracked badly and the road had to be closed and the structure taken down. It was replaced with a rather utilitarian steel girder bridge which was itself destroyed by a German bomb and replaced by a second 'temporary' bridge which remained for some 30 years. The cutting had then to be revetted and a 'modern' bridge replaced it.

155. When the early open-topped omnibuses used this route (*see* plate 128), the legend 'Bus passengers, Low Bridge, remain seated' was a most essential instruction to obey. All subsequent bridges were constructed with the highway statutory clearance of 16½ feet.

156.   This is a view of the old bridge taken from Angel Hill at the end of Sutton Common Road in 1926. The warning notice here seems to be more detailed but far less visible than the brief one shown in plate 155.

157.   The date when the first bridge was built is not known, but this early postcard shows a way down the cutting bank before a bridge existed. Likewise neither the reason for the making of the cutting nor the date of it is known. The commonly-held belief that it was to ease the Prince Regent's journey to Brighton is hardly credible when there are so many greater hills to negotiate on the route.

158. West Street National School photographed in 1870, a few years after it was built. The school consisted of a large room on either side of the head teacher's cottage accommodation; the boys on one side, and girls on the other. There was also a smaller room at the back for infants. In all it provided accommodation for 232 pupils.

159. In 1879 the West Street School was enlarged by adding a wing on each side of the original building, as shown here in the 1920s. This school is where a number of older residents alive today were educated, and it was only demolished in 1971.

160-62. Eversfield School, a private girls' school in Cheam Road in the early part of this century. Eversfield stood almost opposite the Sutton High School for Girls and was described as a 'high class ladies school for resident and non-resident pupils'. Shown here is the main building, with an extension at the rear, the refectory, and (*opposite*) a domestic science class in session. In 1933 the school moved to a large house in Mulgrave Road, where it continued until the outbreak of war. The name Eversfield has been preserved and it is now an old people's home.

163. The Sutton County School for Boys in Throwley Road, built in 1899, remained until the present building in Manor Lane was built in 1928. The building shown here then became the Sutton School of Art for 35 years, which then moved to 'Stowford' in the Brighton Road, until the College of Liberal Arts was built in 1973.

164. Sutton High School for Boys opened in 1879 as a private school in Cambridge House in Cheam Road. It is shown here on a publicity postcard in 1905. The two old chapel buildings on the left were later faced with brick and survived until 1961 when the school closed. The premises were then used for various business purposes until demolished to make way for the new Safeway superstore.

165. Sutton High School for Girls in Park House in Cheam Road, a Girls Public Day School Trust establishment, opened in 1884. Over the years a number of additions were made to the original building and in 1932 Suffolk House next door was purchased as an addition to the school (*see* plate 44).

166. The laboratory of the Girls' High School, at the turn of the century. In those days, nearly a century ago, it was considered very advanced to be teaching science to girls. A more extensive laboratory was built in 1932.

167. Sutton Lodge in Brighton Road, now used as an elderly persons' day centre, was one of the district's ancient farmhouses. It was built in the middle of the 18th century, and for many years was the home of the Overton family. This photograph was taken in 1974.

168. This picture shows the end of the farm cottages and the entrance to the farmyard. The location is the site of Gatton Close.

169. A photograph taken in 1928 in the farmyard, showing the back of the farmhouse through the trees.

170. Another of Sutton's old farms was at the other end of the village beyond the Green. Officially named Hallmead Farm, it was more usually called Skinners Farm after a long-time occupant. Although the farmhouse shown here stood where Hallmead Road is today, the farm lands stretched south-westwards as far as Gander Green Lane, where a cottage known as Skinners Cottage stood near Whittaker Road.

71-73. For Queen Victoria's golden jubilee celebrations in 1887, Oliver Brown the butcher gave the bullock, top left, to be roasted and distributed amongst the old and needy of the town. Its hide was afterwards preserved and stuffed and paraded in high days and carnivals. The picture on the bottom left shows Oliver Brown and his son with the stuffed bull on the occasion of the diamond jubilee in 1897, with a replica of the Victoria cross around its neck – one of which was given to each child instead of the traditional mug which had been given at the golden jubilee. The picture above shows the bullock on a wagon on the occasion of fund-raising for the cottage hospital, c.1909.

174.   The ladies and children of the cricket club outside the pavilion. The date and occasion are unknown, but the hats and costumes suggest *c*.1890.

175.   One of Sutton's cricket teams. There was, of course, the regular Sutton team, but there were at least two other teams: one of shopkeepers from the east side of the High Street and the other from the west side. They played each other at an annual match which, from all accounts, was quite an occasion. It is not known which team this is, but what can be assumed with confidence from the better condition of the thatch on the pavilion roof, is that the photograph was taken some years before the previous picture.

176. A crowd of curious spectators lined the street when a steam traction engine ran out of control into the front room of a cottage 'somewhere in Sutton', *c.*1910.

177. Another road accident, in Cheam Road, *c.*1910, resulted in a fatality.

HANC POLITICS
LETS
BE JOLLY

High Street, Sutton. Xmas Show Week. 1910

1750

S&W. Series.

178.   At each Christmas in the early 1900s the traders in the High Street erected decorations across the street from the Green to the station. This banner of 1910 would be just as apt today.

Bibliography

Bradley, I., Broughton, J., and Cluett, D., *All Our Yesterdays: a pictorial record of the London Borough of Sutton over the past century*, 2nd edn. (1991)

Broughton, J., *The Past in Pictures: a further collection of pictures of the London Borough of Sutton*, 2nd edn. (1991)

Burgess, F., *No Small Change: 100 years of Sutton High Street* (1983)

Burgess, F., *Now and Then: more views of Sutton old and new* (1985)

Church, W. R., *Illustrated Sutton*, 1st edn.(1880)

Marshall, C. J., *History of Cheam and Sutton*, 1st edn.(1936)

Smith, R. P., *A History of Sutton A.D.675-1960*, 1st edn.(1960),